Appetizer
& Snack
Bouquets

Create Your Own Gifts & Centerpieces

Delicious Designs

Printed in China

Published By:

507 Industrial Street
Waverly, IA 50677

ISBN-13: 978-1-56383-400-4
ISBN-10: 1-56383-400-6
Item #3627

Table of Contents

Getting Started 4

Fruit Loops 8

Taco Blooms 12

Escape to Capri 16

Oriental Garden Bundles 20

Bloomin' Tomatoes 24

Coffee Break 27

Stuck on my Honeydew 30

BLT Bouquet 34

Too-Cute Tulips 38

Pinwheel Palooza 42

On a Roll 46

Deli Delight 50

Skinny Dippin' 55

Recipes 58

Getting Started

Serving appetizers and snacks is a great way to start any get-together — and when you display them as beautiful centerpieces or bouquets, guests will admire your handiwork as they mingle around the table. The photos and step-by-step instructions make it easy to create savory or sweet arrangements that are just as delicious as they are impressive. Take an appetizer or snack bouquet to a party or give one as a gift — it's sure to be a hit!

Practice Safety

Wash your hands with soap and water thoroughly and often while handling food. In addition, make sure your work surface is clean and sanitary. Use well-sharpened knives properly with a cutting board underneath and practice general kitchen safety when handling sharp utensils.

Choose the freshest foods available and always wash fresh fruits and vegetables under running water to remove dirt and bacteria. Prior to cutting or peeling, scrub the skin of pineapples, melons or carrots under running water with a vegetable brush. Drain produce and pat dry with paper towels. To keep sliced vegetables fresh and crisp until bouquet assembly, soak them in ice water for 15 minutes or cover with damp paper towels.

For optimal freshness and beauty, serve bouquets promptly after assembly. If holding time in a refrigerator is required, do not add bread items, such as breadsticks, crackers and pretzels, until just before serving. To transport, pack and secure the loosely covered bouquet in a large cooler or box. If given as a gift, encourage the recipient to enjoy it promptly and refrigerate leftovers, removing non-perishable bread items first to prevent sogginess.

Gather Some General Supplies

These supplies may be purchased in kitchen shops, grocery stores and the craft or baking section of most discount stores.

- *Wooden or bamboo skewers, white lollipop or cookie sticks, plastic hors d'oeuvre picks, etc.*

- *Round and flat toothpicks*

- *Styrofoam ("foam")*

- *Food-safe containers, plates and platters*

- *Parchment paper, plastic wrap, waxed paper and aluminum foil*

- *Cutting boards*

- *Knives, such as chef's, paring, serrated, etc.*

- *Crinkle cutter*

- *Cookie cutters (metal and plastic)*

- *Melon baller*

- *Scissors and pizza cutter*

- *Pruning shears*

- *Pastry bags fitted with decorative tips or zippered plastic bags*

- *Rolling pin*

- *Rimmed baking sheets*

- *Nonstick cooking spray*

- *Ribbons, raffia and other embellishments*

Prepare the Base

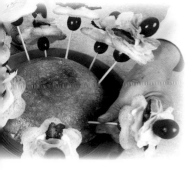

An important part of each appetizer or snack bouquet is choosing a base or container that is both attractive and sturdy. In some cases, the base is a food product that can be eaten along with the skewers of food, such as a loaf of bread on a plate or cherry tomatoes in a vase.

In other bouquets, the base may be a food product that will not be consumed, such as the shell of a melon, head of iceberg lettuce that's trimmed and pressed into a pot or chopped cabbage packed lightly in a vase.

When directions call for a non-edible Styrofoam base, purchase a piece of foam that most closely matches your container's size and shape. It may still need trimming to fit, but that is an easy process. Simply press the container's opening against the foam to make an outline. Cut with a knife, about ½″ inside the outline. Trim foam as needed so it fits into container with a little space to spare. Generally, the height of the foam should be about 1″ shorter than the top of the container, unless directed differently for a specific bouquet.

Wrap foam in aluminum foil to prevent contact with food. Test the fit again; covered foam should fit snugly in container for a stable and secure bouquet. The foil can be disguised by arranging another food over the top, such as nuts, coffee beans or leafy greens like kale.

Plan your arrangements based on the size of your container and the number of guests you plan to serve. Use the photos for ideas and then personalize your bouquets by choosing skewer lengths and placements that work for you. Think about the season or party theme when choosing containers and pick colors that complement the appetizers or snacks.

Place the Foods

A variety of skewers can be used to display foods, such as plain or frill toothpicks, bamboo or plastic cocktail picks and white lollipop or cookie sticks. Common wooden or bamboo skewers, 10˝ to 12˝ long, are inexpensive, versatile and easy to find. They can be trimmed to desired lengths with clean, sanitary pruning shears. They can also be inserted into green onion stems to resemble real flower stems.

In most cases, it's best to slide food onto the pointed end of a skewer and poke the blunt end into the base, unless directed otherwise. If necessary, make starter holes with a toothpick or skewer point.

Some foods tend to slide down a long skewer after assembly. To prevent this, place a "stopper," such as a raisin or small piece of bell pepper, on the skewer before adding the appetizers.

Fruit
Loops

Celebrate summertime with disks of chilled cantaloupe, watermelon and honeydew.

You will need:

1 head iceberg lettuce
Container (Sample uses a ceramic pot, 4½″ in diameter and 4″ deep.)
1 large cantaloupe
1 medium honeydew melon
½ small seedless watermelon

Round cookie cutters (1¾″, 2″, 2¾″, 3½″)
20 (10″) wooden or bamboo skewers
1 small bunch curly parsley

To Begin...

1) Place iceberg lettuce into container, trimming it as needed to achieve a snug fit.

2) Slice off a narrow piece of melon from the stem end. Slice off the cantaloupe rind, removing all green from the orange flesh. Then cut another crosswise slice from end, ½″ thick.

3) Cut 2 or 3 (½"-thick) slices from one side of the cantaloupe until center cavity is reached. In the same way, make 2 or 3 (½"-thick) slices on the opposite side of cantaloupe. Repeat to cut ½"-thick slices from remaining 2 sides of cantaloupe.

4) With narrowest side of each melon slice facing up, use cookie cutters to cut out flat disks of cantaloupe. Use the largest cutters that will fit on each slice first; then cut a variety of smaller disks from remaining melon. Arrange cantaloupe disks on a rimmed baking sheet and refrigerate. Discard seeds and reserve any cantaloupe scraps for another use. Prepare and cut honeydew melon as directed in steps 2-4.

5) Cut watermelon into ½"-thick slices, leaving rind intact. Use cookie cutters of varying sizes to cut out disks from the pink flesh. Arrange watermelon disks on a rimmed baking sheet and refrigerate.

6) To assemble skewers of fruit, insert the pointed end of a skewer into the edge of a melon disk, gently pressing it through the fruit and stopping about 1″ from opposite edge *(do not pierce top edge)*. Thread 1 extra-large or large melon disk on 7 or 8 skewers.

Thread 1 or 2 medium and small disks on 7 or 8 skewers. Thread 2 to 5 of the smallest disks on remaining skewers, using a combination of honeydew, cantaloupe and watermelon.

7) To arrange the bouquet, push blunt end of skewers firmly into lettuce base until pieces are straight and secure. Start by inserting largest melon disks in the center of bouquet, trimming skewers as needed to get a variety of heights. *(The largest disks generally need shorter skewers for stability.)*

Insert skewers with next largest disks at the sides and in back of largest pieces, varying the heights. Fill in empty spaces with skewers of smaller disks until bouquet looks balanced. In some spaces, it may be easier to remove melon disks while inserting skewers and then replace the fruit after skewers are secure.

8) Cover lettuce base with pieces of parsley, tucking them into bouquet with a skewer as needed. Refrigerate bouquet until serving, up to 3 hours.

Taco Blooms

Let the fiesta begin with
this colorful layered dip
and tortilla chips.

You will need:

- 1 (10") sun-dried tomato basil flour tortilla (or more)
- 1 (10") garden spinach herb flour tortilla (or more)
- Leaf-shaped cookie cutter (3" to 4")
- 2 tsp. olive oil
- Salt to taste
- 1 (16 oz.) can refried beans
- 1 (1 oz.) pkg. taco seasoning mix
- 1 ripe avocado*
- ½ (1 oz.) pkg. guacamole seasoning mix
- 1⅓ C. sour cream, divided
- Pastry bag, fitted with large open star tip
- 6 oz. cream cheese, softened
- Large platter (Sample uses a 13" charger.)
- 1¼ C. chunky salsa, divided
- 1 C. shredded Cheddar cheese, divided
- 1 Roma tomato, chopped and drained
- 4 green onions, sliced
- Scoop-type tortilla chips, divided
- 1 (2.25 oz.) can sliced black olives, drained

To Begin...

1) Preheat oven to 400°. Line a large baking sheet with parchment paper; set aside.

2) Stack tomato basil and spinach herb tortillas together, edges even. Press a leaf cookie cutter firmly through both layers to cut out 2 leaf shapes; repeat to make about 14 leaves. Arrange leaves in a single layer on prepared baking sheet and brush tops with oil. Bake for 4 to 5 minutes or until edges just begin to brown. Remove from oven and sprinkle with salt; let cool on pan.

3) In a medium bowl, stir together refried beans and taco seasoning mix; let stand for 15 minutes to blend flavors. In a small bowl, mash avocado flesh and stir in guacamole seasoning until well blended; cover and refrigerate at least 15 minutes. Place ⅓ cup sour cream into a pastry bag fitted with a large open star tip; reserve in refrigerator for piping. Whisk together remaining 1 cup sour cream and cream cheese until blended; set aside.

4) Reserve ⅓ cup bean mixture to fill scoops. Spread remaining bean mixture in an 8″ circle over the center of platter. Spread sour cream mixture over beans.

5) Spread avocado mixture over creamy layer. Top with about 1 cup salsa followed by ¾ cup Cheddar cheese, tomato and green onions; press lightly to hold in place.

6) Spoon 1 teaspoon reserved bean mixture into about 15 tortilla chips. Top each chip with a sprinkling of remaining Cheddar cheese. Spoon ½ teaspoon of remaining salsa over cheese.

7) With reserved pastry bag, pipe a sour cream flower on each filled chip. Top with a sliced olive.

8) Arrange chip "flowers" over layered mixtures on platter.

9) Arrange tortilla leaves around edge of platter. Serve promptly with remaining tortilla chips.

*Avocado Prep

Cut avocado lengthwise around the seed. Twist halves apart to expose pit. Poke a knife edge into the pit and twist to remove. Cut through avocado flesh in both directions without cutting the skin. Flex skin slightly and scoop out diced flesh with a spoon.

Escape to Capri

A taste of Italy—tortellini, mozzarella cheese, tomatoes, black olives and herbed breadsticks.

You will need:

No-Knead Bread Dough
(recipe on page 58)*

Olive oil

Grated Parmesan cheese

Coarse salt

Italian seasoning

8 oz. fresh mozzarella
cheese

1 green bell pepper,
cored and seeded

30 frozen cheese tortellini,
plain and/or spinach
flavor (about 1½ cups)

16 to 20 large pitted black
olives, drained
(about 3 oz.)

1 bunch fresh basil leaves,
rinsed and patted dry

1 pt. red grape tomatoes

1 pt. yellow cherry tomatoes

1 (14 oz.) can artichoke
hearts, drained and
sliced, optional

16 to 20 (10˝) wooden or
bamboo skewers

Container (Sample uses
a 3 x 3½˝ rectangular
glass vase, 7˝ deep.)

Italian Dipping Sauce
(recipe on page 19)

*You may also use 8 to 10
purchased breadsticks.*

To Begin...

1) Prepare No-Knead
Bread Dough with
olive oil according to recipe
on page 58. Let rise for
2 hours.

2) Preheat oven to 375°.
Line a baking sheet with
aluminum foil and brush
with olive oil; set aside. Snip
off a ball of dough the size
of a large orange (about
½ pound). Sprinkle with
flour, stretch and shape
dough into a smooth ball. On
a floured surface, roll out to
a 7 x 10˝ rectangle. Brush
with olive oil; sprinkle with
Parmesan cheese, salt and
Italian seasoning to taste.

③ With a pizza cutter, slice the length of dough into ¼″-wide strips.

④ Arrange strips on prepared baking sheet, stretching slightly; twist or shape one end of each strip as desired so finished breadsticks are 8″ to 10″ long. Bake for 10 to 12 minutes or until golden brown. Cool completely.

⑤ Cut mozzarella cheese into ½″ to ¾″ cubes; set aside. Cut green pepper into 1″ pieces; set aside. Cook tortellini in boiling water as directed on package. Rinse in cool water, drain and set aside.

⑥ To assemble bouquet, slide a piece of green pepper onto the pointed end of each skewer, followed by 1 or 2 tortellini, a black olive, cheese cube and tomato. Add sliced artichoke hearts, if desired. Alternate the order of items but always place the green pepper "stopper" first to anchor other foods. Top most of the skewers with tomatoes; top remaining skewers with cheese.

7) Fill the vase partway with some of remaining tomatoes, Arrange skewers in vase, starting around the edges first. Place sticks at an angle toward the center, between tomatoes without piercing them. Add more tomatoes to vase. Arrange remaining skewers to fill center section of vase.

8) Place breadsticks between skewers until bouquet looks full. Serve promptly with Italian Dipping Sauce to drizzle over skewers and breadsticks.

Italian Dipping Sauce

In a small bowl, whisk together ¼ cup olive oil, ¼ cup balsamic or red wine vinegar, 1 tablespoon chopped fresh basil, ¼ teaspoon dry oregano, 1½ teaspoons finely minced garlic, ¼ teaspoon coarse salt and dash of pepper. For a quicker dipping sauce, use bottled Italian salad dressing.

Oriental Garden Bundles

A crunchy new twist on shrimp-filled spring rolls.

You will need:

10 thin 6½″ egg roll/spring
roll wrappers (from a
16 oz. pkg.)

Toothpicks

Parchment paper

3 T. light soy sauce, divided

2 T. rice vinegar or white
wine vinegar

6 T. apple cider

½ tsp. grated gingerroot

20 large, fully-cooked
frozen shrimp, thawed

1 medium cucumber, peeled,
seeded and chopped

1 medium carrot, julienned*

2 green onions, chopped

2 T. stir fry sauce

2 T. creamy peanut butter

2 C. shredded leaf lettuce

¼ C. chopped fresh cilantro,
plus whole leaves for
garnishing

Container (Sample uses
a 5″ square metal pot,
5″ deep.)

Sweet and sour sauce,
optional

To Begin…

1) Preheat oven to 400°. Line a baking sheet with
parchment paper; set aside.

2) Working with one
egg roll wrapper at
a time, roll wrapper into
a cone shape, overlapping
two opposite corners in
front, with one corner at
the top and the point of the
cone at the bottom. Fasten
overlapping layers together
with a toothpick.

3) Crumple small pieces
of parchment paper
and gently tuck inside cone
to hold it open. Set cone on a
paper plate and microwave
on high for 30 to 45 seconds
or until firm. Let cool slightly
and remove parchment
paper. Reuse crumpled paper

for additional cones. Transfer cones to prepared baking sheet and spray generously with nonstick cooking spray. Bake for 2 to 3 minutes or until light golden brown around edges. Cool slightly before removing toothpicks; then cool completely.

4) In a medium bowl, stir together 2 tablespoons soy sauce, rice vinegar, apple cider and gingerroot.

5) Remove tails from shrimp and rinse with cold water. Chop 10 shrimp and place in bowl with soy sauce mixture. Add cucumber, carrot and green onion; toss to coat. Marinate in refrigerator for 15 minutes, stirring several times. Reserve remaining whole shrimp for garnishes.

6) In a small bowl, combine stir fry sauce, peanut butter and remaining 1 tablespoon soy sauce; whisk until smooth. Spread a spoonful of peanut sauce inside each baked cone.

7) Drain marinated shrimp mixture, reserving sauce for serving. Fill each cone with a portion of the lettuce, chopped cilantro and shrimp mixture.

8) Top with more lettuce, cilantro leaves and 1 reserved whole shrimp.

9) Place crinkled aluminum foil in the bottom of container as needed. Arrange cones in container, gently pressing ends into foil for support and placement. Serve with sweet and sour sauce and/or remaining soy sauce marinade for dipping.

*To Julienne Carrots

Peel the carrot and cut off a thin lengthwise slice to make a flat side. Cut into 2″ lengths. Place pieces flat side down and cut into thin lengthwise slices. Stack several slices together and cut again to make thin matchstick strips.

Bloomin'
Tomatoes

Creamy fillings in cherry tomatoes for bite-size appetizers.

You will need:

35 to 40 red cherry tomatoes

6 oz. cream cheese, softened, divided

½ C. shredded smoked Gouda cheese, room temperature

2 T. butter, softened

1 T. milk

½ tsp. steak sauce

Pastry bags fitted with large open star tips

½ ripe avocado, pitted, peeled and diced

1½ T. basil pesto

1 tsp. lemon juice

1 head iceberg lettuce

Container (Sample uses a ceramic bowl, 7½″ in diameter and 3″ deep.)

1 small bunch green kale

Toothpicks

To Begin...

1) With a sharp knife, cut a thin slice off the top of each tomato. Cut around the inside to loosen flesh. With a small spoon or melon baller, carefully scoop out seeds and soft flesh to make a hollow cavity. Set tomatoes, cut side down, on a baking sheet lined with paper towels; let stand for 30 minutes to drain.

2) To make smoked cheese filling, in a small mixing bowl, combine 4 ounces cream cheese, Gouda cheese and butter. Mash to blend. Add milk and steak sauce; beat on medium speed until fluffy. Spoon mixture into a pastry bag fitted with a large open star tip and set aside.

3 To make avocado-basil filling, in another small bowl, combine avocado, remaining 2 ounces cream cheese, pesto and lemon juice. Mash well and whisk until smooth. Spoon filling into another pastry bag fitted with a large open star tip; set aside.

4 Set lettuce into container and trim off bottom slightly so top of lettuce mounds about 2″ above rim. Tuck pieces of kale around the edges, between container and lettuce.

5 Insert a toothpick into the center top of lettuce until ¾″ of pick remains visible. Gently press the bottom of 1 tomato onto toothpick, hollow side up. Insert a row of toothpicks into lettuce around center tomato and attach a tomato to each pick. Working in a circular pattern, insert additional toothpicks into lettuce and attach remaining tomatoes to cover lettuce.

6 Pipe fillings into tomatoes, alternating colors as desired*. Serve promptly or refrigerate for up to 2 hours before serving.

To stuff all tomatoes with a single flavor of filling, double the appropriate filling ingredients.

Coffee Break

Take a break with
dressed-up donut holes.

You will need:

Styrofoam

Container (Sample uses a large mug, 4˝ in diameter and 4˝ deep.)

¼ C. pink candy wafers (18 pieces)

2 small zippered plastic bags

18 donut holes (glazed, sugared and/or powder sugared)

¼ C. chocolate candy wafers (18 pieces)

White lollipop sticks (8˝, 4˝)

Plain or chocolate-covered coffee beans (.15 lbs.)

6 to 8 (5˝) strawberry covered biscuit sticks (Sample uses Pocky sticks, available in the Oriental section of most grocery stores.)

Flat toothpicks, optional

Ribbon and bow, optional

Double-sided tape, optional

To Begin...

1) Cut Styrofoam to fit into mug, ending 1˝ below top of mug. Wrap foam in aluminum foil and place in mug; set aside.

2) Melt pink candy wafers in a microwave-safe bowl following package instructions; stir until smooth. Spoon warm melted candy into a zippered plastic bag, pressing it to one corner. Snip off a tiny piece of the corner to create a "tip" for piping. Gently squeeze bag to pipe melted pink candy back and forth over 6 donut holes. Let dry on waxed paper. In the same way, melt chocolate candy wafers until smooth and use another plastic bag to pipe chocolate over 5 or 6 additional donut holes. Let dry.

3 Insert 1 (8″) lollipop stick into the donut hole you want in the center of bouquet. Insert the other end of stick into the center of foam until secure. If necessary, trim off 1″ from end of stick to achieve the right height.

4 Trim 6 (8″) skewers to a length of 6″ to 6½″. Insert each trimmed stick into a donut hole. Press other end of stick into foam, arranging stems around the tall center donut as desired.

5 Cover base with coffee beans. Avoiding the beans, insert approximately 10 (4″) lollipop sticks into foam around the edge of mug, tilting slightly outward and spacing sticks ¾″ apart. Gently press a donut hole halfway onto each stick, allowing donuts to touch. (If necessary, remove some upper donut holes to make placement of bottom row easier; then replace on sticks.)

6 Insert biscuit sticks into coffee beans or foam between donuts to fill empty spaces in bouquet. If sticks need to be taller, gently twist the small end of a toothpick into uncoated end of biscuit stick; then press other end of toothpick into foam.

7 If desired, tie a ribbon and bow around mug, securing with double-sided tape.

Stuck on my Honeydew

Fruit and cheese kababs add fun to any party.

You will need:

Melon baller

½ honeydew melon (cut crosswise), seeded

½ cantaloupe, seeded

1 small head iceberg lettuce

2 (½″-thick) crosswise slices from a whole fresh pineapple

Small metal cookie cutters (1½″ heart, 1″ square, 1″ round, 1¼″ diamond)

3 (12 oz.) blocks cheese, 1″ thick (Sample uses Cheddar, Colby-Jack and mozzarella.)

1 bunch red seedless grapes (45 to 50)

1 bunch green seedless grapes (45 to 50)

5 (10″) wooden or bamboo skewers

75 to 80 (4″) party picks

Large plate (Sample uses a 10″ round glass plate.)

To Begin...

1) With a melon baller, cut small and large balls from the flesh of honeydew melon, making as many as you can; set balls on a rimmed baking sheet and refrigerate until assembly. With a large spoon, scrape out remaining flesh, leaving a melon shell about

½″ thick. Pat shell dry with paper towels; set aside. Cut additional small and large balls from cantaloupe flesh; place on rimmed baking sheet and refrigerate.

2) Peel off outer leaves of lettuce and trim head as needed until it fits snugly inside melon shell.

3) With lettuce inside shell, carefully slice lettuce so its cut edge is level with cut edge of melon.

4) To cut a pineapple heart, place cookie cutter on 1 pineapple slice, with point toward core and curved edges near pineapple skin. (Metal cookie cutters are recommended for a clean, even cut.) Press straight down on the cookie cutter, using even pressure. Remove pineapple heart from cutter. Repeat to cut 6 to 7 hearts from each pineapple slice. Place hearts on a rimmed baking sheet and refrigerate until assembly.

5) Cut through the 1″ thickness of each block of cheese using the square*, round and diamond cookie cutters to make "plugs" of each shape. With a sharp knife, slice plugs in half to ½″ thickness. Cover cheese until assembly.

6) Just before assembly, pat fruits dry with paper towels. Trim 1 skewer to 8″ long. Insert the point through 3 alternating pineapple hearts and grapes; set aside.

*If a square cutter is not available, cut cheese into 1″ cubes with a knife.

7) Using the 4″ picks, make skewers of fruit and/or cheese, alternating pieces as desired. Avoid placing melon and cheese on the same skewer. Make half of the picks with 3 items and remaining picks with 2 items. Grapes and cheese shapes may be skewered lengthwise or crosswise. Allow at least ½″ of exposed pick at each end: one end to poke into the base and the other end for guests to hold.

8) Set melon/lettuce base on the plate, cut side down. With a skewer point, make a starter hole in center top of melon, avoiding the stem; press reserved 8″ pineapple heart/grape skewer into hole. Insert a row of 18 to 20 (3-item) picks around the bottom of melon, about ½″ from cut edge. Repeat with a row of 2-item picks, 1″ above first row, staggering them between previous picks. Insert additional rows of 2- and 3-item picks to cover melon, but leave about 1″ of open space remaining around tall center skewer.

9) Trim 3″ to 4″ off blunt end of remaining 4 skewers. Make starter holes in open space around top of melon; push trimmed end of skewers into holes to desired height. Thread fruit and cheese onto exposed skewers, sliding pieces down toward melon. Fill any open space with remaining short picks. Serve promptly or refrigerate for up to 1 hour before serving.

BLT Bouquet

The bacon-lettuce-and-tomato sandwich just got better!

You will need:

No-Knead Bread Dough
 (recipe on page 58)*
Vegetable oil
Round oven-safe bowl
 (6″ to 7″ in diameter)
1 egg
20 slices white bread
Flower-shaped cookie
 cutters (3″, 2″)
28 to 34 (10″) wooden or
 bamboo skewers
10 slices thick-cut bacon

6 (1/8″-thick) slices
 provolone or American
 cheese, optional
1 pt. yellow cherry
 tomatoes (about 20)
1/2 head iceberg lettuce
Mayonnaise
2 pts. red grape tomatoes
 (about 45)
Large plate (Sample
 uses a 9″ round
 ceramic plate.)

*You may also purchase a 1-pound round
 loaf of dense bakery or artisan bread.*

To Begin...

1) Prepare No-Knead Bread Dough with *olive oil*
 according to recipe on page 58. Let rise for 2 hours.

2) To make 1 round loaf, use half of prepared dough
 (about 1 pound). Dust dough with flour and shape
 into a ball, stretching the top smooth and tucking it
 under the bottom. Oil an oven-proof bowl and place
 dough in bowl, smooth side down. Cover with lightly-
 oiled plastic wrap; let rest in a warm place for
 1 hour. (If dough is refrigerated, let it rest for 1½ hours.)

3) Preheat oven to 350°.
 Uncover bowl and
 bake bread for 35 minutes
 or until lightly browned
 and firm. Meanwhile, whisk
 egg with 1 tablespoon water.
 Remove bread from bowl and
 invert onto an ungreased

baking sheet; brush top (the side shaped like the bowl) with egg mixture. Return to oven to bake for 10 minutes more. Let bread cool completely before assembling bouquet.

4) Decrease oven temperature to 375°. With the 3″ cookie cutter, cut flowers from 20 slices of bread. Use a skewer to poke a small starter hole in the center of each flower. Bake flowers on an ungreased baking sheet for 12 minutes or until crisp and light golden brown. Cool completely.

5) Cut bacon strips crosswise into 3 pieces (about 3″ long). In a large skillet, fry bacon on both sides until almost crisp; drain on paper towels.

6) With the 2″ cookie cutter, cut flowers from provolone and/or American cheese, if desired. Set aside.

7) Cut lettuce into small wedges. Spread mayonnaise on the center of each bread flower.

8) To make BLT skewers, slide a small grape tomato on the pointed end of a skewer followed by a bread flower, cheese flower (if desired), 1 or 2 pieces of bacon and lettuce wedge. Finish with another tomato but do not pierce the top.

9) Make 7 or 8 skewers of yellow cherry tomatoes, placing 2 or 3 tomatoes on each skewer without piercing the top tomato; set aside.

10) For the base, place round loaf of bread on the serving plate. To assemble bouquet, trim 6 to 8 BLT skewers to 5″ lengths; insert these skewers into the loaf around lower edge. Trim another group of BLT skewers to 6½″ lengths and insert into bread above first row. Insert remaining long BLT skewers into top section of bread, trimming skewers as needed for a balanced bouquet. Fill in empty spaces with yellow tomato skewers. Serve promptly.

Prepare loaf of bread at least 4 hours ahead of time or the day before assembling bouquet.

Garnishing Tip

With 1½″ or 2″ cookie cutters, cut small flowers from additional slices of bread. Bake at 375° for 10 to 12 minutes. Set flowers around loaf base to garnish bouquet. These flowers may also be served with the Party Cheeseball on page 60.

Too-Cute Tulips

*Tiptoe through the tulips,
asparagus and green onions
for crunchy goodness.*

You will need:

- 1 (16 oz.) pkg. large red radishes (about 20), room temperature
- 2 bunches medium green onions
- 6 to 10 fresh asparagus spears
- ½ head red cabbage

- Container (Sample uses a glass vase, 3½″ in diameter and 9″ tall.)
- 15 (12″) wooden or bamboo skewers
- 10 to 15 (10″) wooden or bamboo skewers

To Begin...

1) With a small sharp knife, slice off the stem end of a radish so it will rest flat on a cutting board. Cut a V-shaped wedge from center top of radish by slicing the first side of the "V" about ¼″ deep and then making an opposing cut until root can be removed.

2) Cut out 2 more V-shaped wedges from top of radish, positioning them like an "X" over the first wedge, to make a 6-pointed star.

3) To cut "petals," insert knife point about ⅛″ below a red peak. Make one shallow slice down the radish under the peak, angling knife toward the center like half of another V-shape while following the line of the peak. About ¼″ from the bottom of radish, gently withdraw knife to stop the cut. To make the other half of the same petal, re-insert knife tip so it intersects

the top of the first cut. Make another shallow, angled slice down radish under the peak on the other side to complete the "V", stopping near the bottom as before. Do not connect the bottom cuts or the petal will fall off radish. Petals should be a bit loose to the touch. Repeat process to make 1 petal under each peak. Gently bend petals outward and place radish in ice water for 1 or 2 hours or overnight. Repeat steps 1-3 to make 15 radish tulips. (For convenience, make radish tulips the day before assembly.)

4 To make green onion frills, slice off root of each onion. Make 3 thin lengthwise cuts through the white bulb end of onion, about 1¼″ long. Roll onion a quarter turn (to uncut side) and slice once or twice more. Trim frills to 4″ lengths. Place frilled pieces in ice water for at least 1 hour; reserve green stems for step 8.

5 Trim 1″ off thick ends of asparagus spears. To parcook, wrap spears in wet paper towels and microwave for 1½ minutes. Let cool slightly, unwrap and rinse in cool water; place in ice water.

6 Slice and coarsely chop cabbage. Place in vase, filling about ⅔ full.

7 Cut off bulb end of remaining onions and reserve for another use. Separate the long green stems. Gently slide 12″ skewers into either end of larger onion stems to cover. Slide 10″ skewers into smaller stems.

8 Slide 10″ skewers into thick end of asparagus spears as far as possible without splitting spears.

9 Slide 10″ skewers into cut end of onion frills (toward frilled end) until secure.

10 Arrange the longest skewers in the vase (for tulips), pushing blunt ends into cabbage until secure. Press radish tulips onto skewer points and arrange "flowers", trimming skewers as needed until bouquet looks balanced. Work from the back of bouquet toward the front. Add asparagus spears and onion frills to complete the bouquet, trimming skewers as needed. Bouquet can be refrigerated for up to 2 hours before serving*.

*Just before serving, spritz or brush radishes with water.

Pinwheel Palooza

Hearty tortilla rolls, pretty enough to eat.

You will need:

Sheet of Styrofoam, 2″ thick

Container (Sample uses a 7 x 9″ metal platter, 1½″ deep.)

Tacky mounting putty

⅓ C. mayonnaise

2 cloves garlic, minced

3 (10″) sun-dried tomato basil flour tortillas

1 C. fresh spinach leaves, stems trimmed

6 thin slices deli roast beef

6 thin slices provolone cheese

1 large tomato, thinly sliced

1 C. chopped fresh broccoli

4 oz. cream cheese, softened

1 tsp. dried dillweed

1½ tsp. lemon juice

¼ tsp. paprika

¼ tsp. garlic salt

Pepper to taste

1 medium carrot, grated

¼ C. finely chopped green bell pepper

⅓ C. frozen peas, thawed

3 (10″) garden spinach herb flour tortillas

40 wooden or bamboo skewers and cocktail picks (4″ to 10″ long)

1 small bunch green kale

To Begin...

1) Cut Styrofoam to fit container and wrap in aluminum foil. Attach foam base to bottom of container with mounting putty; set aside.

2) In a small bowl, mix mayonnaise and garlic; spread thinly on one side of each tomato basil tortilla to within 1″ of edges. Top with spinach leaves and a layer of roast beef (2 pieces per tortilla). Arrange provolone cheese and tomato slices over center of meat. Roll up tortillas tightly and set on a plate, seam side down. Refrigerate for 30 minutes.

3 Microwave broccoli with 2 tablespoons water for 1½ minutes or until slightly tender. Rinse in cold water, drain and set aside.

4 In a medium bowl, mix cream cheese, dillweed, lemon juice, paprika, garlic salt and pepper. Spread a thin layer on one side of each spinach herb tortilla to within 1″ of edges. Sprinkle with an even amount of carrot, bell pepper, peas and broccoli. Roll up tortillas tightly and set on a plate, seam side down. Refrigerate 30 minutes.

5 Trim 1″ off each end of tortilla rolls; discard. Slice remaining rolls crosswise to make pinwheels, about 1″ wide. Cut approximately 7 pinwheels from each tortilla roll.

6 Cover foam base with kale, using toothpicks as needed to hold in place.

7) Make 4 or 5 double pinwheels by inserting the pointed end of a 10″ skewer through 2 contrasting pinwheels, without piercing the top edge of upper pinwheels. Make single pinwheels of shorter lengths, trimming 1″ to 3″ off blunt end of 10″ skewers as needed. If using 4″ cocktail picks for the pinwheels in front, push the picks all the way through, from top to bottom with the "handle" on top.

8) Push blunt end of skewers into the base, arranging the double pinwheels across the center first. Place next-longest skewers at angles, pointing outward from each double pinwheel, to create 3 or 4 "bunches." Arrange shorter skewers vertically or at angles in empty spaces. Finish by placing shortest picks around the edges. Refrigerate for up to 3 hours before serving.

Variations

Use whole wheat or flour tortillas for pinwheels. Add these to the bouquet as a third color or use them in place of colored tortillas.

Prepare and use other fillings as desired, such as the Shrimp Filling on page 59.

On a Roll

Tiny cinnamon rolls and candied pecans—perfect for snacking or brunch.

You will need:

No-Knead Bread Dough
(recipe on page 58)*

1 egg white

½ C. plus 2 T. brown
sugar, divided

¼ tsp. vanilla extract

4 C. whole pecans

3½ T. sugar, divided

1½ tsp. ground
cinnamon, divided

Container (Sample uses a
5″ round tin, 2″ deep.)

Sheet of Styrofoam
(1⅛″ thick)

40 (3″) cinnamon sticks

Low-temperature glue gun

Raffia

¼ C. butter, melted

Unflavored dental
floss or string

30 (10″) wooden or
bamboo skewers

Buttercream Frosting
(recipe on page 59) or
1 C. canned frosting

*You may also purchase 28 to 30 small snack-size
cinnamon rolls.

To Begin...

1) Prepare No-Knead Bread Dough with *vegetable oil*
according to recipe on page 58. Let rise for 2 hours.

2) Meanwhile, prepare
candied pecans to cover
base. Preheat oven to 300°.
Line a baking sheet with
waxed paper and spray with
nonstick cooking spray; set
aside. In a medium mixing
bowl, beat egg white on high
speed until stiff peaks form.
Stir in ½ cup brown sugar

and vanilla until smooth. Stir in pecans until coated.
Spread on prepared baking sheet and bake for
15 minutes. In a small bowl, mix 1½ tablespoons sugar
and ½ teaspoon cinnamon. Remove pecans from oven
and stir to separate. Sprinkle with cinnamon-sugar;
toss to coat. Return pan to oven for 3 minutes. Cool
completely. (Use about 1 cup pecans for bouquet; serve
remaining nuts on the side or reserve for another use.)

3 When ready to bake rolls, preheat oven to 350°. Line a baking sheet with aluminum foil and spray with nonstick cooking spray; set aside.

4 Snip off a ball of prepared dough the size of a large orange (about ½ pound). Sprinkle with flour, stretch and shape dough into a smooth ball. On a floured surface, roll out to a thin 7 x 12″ rectangle. In a small bowl, stir together remaining 2 tablespoons sugar, 2 tablespoons brown sugar and 1 teaspoon cinnamon. Spread half the melted butter over dough. Sprinkle with half the sugar mixture.

5 Starting at one long edge, roll up dough tightly to make a log; pinch long edge to seal. Use floss to cut dough into ¾″-wide slices (14 to 15 slices). Place slices on prepared baking sheet and flatten to ½″ thickness. If desired, pinch opposite edges to make a few "leaf" shapes. Repeat steps 4-5 with another piece of dough. (For a larger bouquet, make additional rolls and increase amount of frosting.)

6 Bake rolls for 15 to 18 minutes or until golden brown. Remove from pan and let cool.

7) Cut Styrofoam to fit container, with top resting just below top edge of container. Wrap foam in aluminum foil and place in container. With a glue gun, attach cinnamon sticks vertically to the side of container, placing ends even with bottom and lining up sticks until covered. Tie raffia around the outside.

8) To assemble bouquet, insert pointed end of skewers into one edge of each cinnamon roll without piercing the top (unless placing more than 1 roll on a skewer). Trim skewers as needed to get different lengths. Insert blunt end of longest skewers in the center area of foam base first. Arrange medium skewers at angles pointing outward from the center. Place shorter skewers toward the front and back of arrangement to fill bouquet. When you like the arrangement, pipe or spread Buttercream Frosting (recipe on page 59) on approximately 12 cinnamon rolls. If preferred, slide those rolls off their skewers, frost them and then carefully replace frosted rolls on skewers. Extra frosting may be served with the bouquet.

9) Cover base with prepared candied pecans before serving.

Deli
Delight

A basket full of crowd-pleasing meat, cheese and veggie hors d'oeuvres.

You will need:

- 30 round thin deli slices ham, turkey and hard salami*
- 20 thin slices provolone, Colby-Jack and/or American cheese*
- 2 stalks celery, ends removed
- 6 radishes
- 25 to 30 (10″) wooden or bamboo skewers
- 2 to 3 medium carrots, peeled
- Crinkle cutter
- Wood and/or plastic toothpicks
- 2 medium cucumbers
- Melon baller
- 4 yellow or red cherry tomatoes, optional
- 15 medium pitted black olives, drained
- 8 to 10 large stuffed green olives, drained, divided
- 12 to 15 red grape tomatoes
- Container (Sample uses a 9″ round basket, 3″ deep.)
- 2 heads iceberg lettuce
- 1 small bunch green kale
- Flower-shaped cookie cutter (3″)
- Spreadable chive and onion cream cheese, room temperature
- 6 to 8 sweet gherkin pickles, drained
- 6 to 8 whole cobs baby corn, drained
- 6 pretzel rods

*Allow meat and cheese to stand at room temperature for 30 minutes for easier handling.

To Begin...

1) To make celery curls, cut celery stalks into finger lengths; split pieces in half lengthwise. With a sharp knife, make parallel lengthwise cuts through each piece, starting about 1″ from an end and placing cuts very close together. Chill in ice water for 2 hours or until curled.

2) To prepare radish wheels, slice off stem and root of each radish, leaving a small white circle on the top and bottom. Cutting at an angle, slice out small V-shaped wedges of red skin, running between top and bottom of radish; remove wedges. Space wedges evenly to show white stripes. Poke the point of a skewer into the edge of each radish wheel; cover with damp paper towels.

3) Cut thickest end of carrots into 5″ lengths. With a crinkle cutter, slice each length into 4 even spears. Poke a toothpick into the large end of each carrot spear; wrap in damp paper towels.

4) Cut off 1¼″ from both ends of cucumbers; reserve center part of cucumber for another use. With a melon baller, remove insides of cucumber ends to make shells. With a sharp knife, cut out 5 evenly spaced triangles from the edge of each shell to create "flower petals." Round off the corners of each petal and trim out excess flesh. Fasten a cherry tomato in the center by inserting a toothpick from bottom of shell into tomato without piercing the top. Cover with damp paper towels.

5) Make several skewers of black olives; make other skewers of green olives with grape tomatoes, reserving some for meat and cheese flowers. Cover with damp paper towels.

6) Line basket with waxed paper. Place both heads of lettuce in basket, cutting 1 head as needed for a snug fit. Lettuce should mound above top of basket slightly. Arrange kale over lettuce.

7) With the cookie cutter, cut half of cheese slices into flower shapes. Bouquet flowers can be made with various combinations of meat and cheese and a small amount of cream cheese spread between the layers. Stack 1 or 2 meat slices with 1 cheese slice, staggering top edges. (Cheese may be on the top or bottom.) Push the point of a skewer into one end of the following center items: pickle, corn, green olive or grape tomato. Place the skewered item on the center of a meat/cheese stack and fold lower edges over each other to form a cone shape with skewer sticking out the bottom. Fasten overlapping layers in front with a toothpick. Make about 18 skewers this way.

8) For remaining 6 to 8 flowers, wrap the meat/cheese layers around an unskewered center item and shape the cone, but push a skewer point through the whole flower at an angle to hold it together. Cover all cones with waxed paper to prevent drying.

9) Fold 1 piece of salami in half, about ¾″ off center. Roll it into a small cone, cut edges up. Wrap a second slice of salami around cone so upper edge flairs out like a flower, folding up bottom edge to enclose cone and finish rosette; fasten with a toothpick.

10) Gather prepared skewers. Begin bouquet assembly by inserting skewers of meat and cheese flowers into base, trimming skewers as needed so flowers rest low in bouquet. Place them in different directions so arrangement is attractive from all sides.

11) Place cucumber flowers low in bouquet, pressing toothpicks into base. Fill open spaces of bouquet with carrot spears, radish wheels, pretzel rods** and skewers of olives and tomatoes. Drain celery curls, insert toothpicks and add to bouquet as desired. Serve promptly.

** Break off one end of each pretzel rod and gently twist a toothpick into broken end so pretzel can be inserted into base more securely.

Skinny Dippin'

A garden of crisp vegetables and dip—a colorful low-cal snack or appetizer.

You will need:

10 large red radishes

6 to 8 stalks celery, divided

8 to 10 fresh asparagus spears

1 bunch green onions

1 stalk fresh broccoli

3 large bell peppers (Sample uses 1 yellow, 1 green and 1 red.)

4 to 5 medium carrots, peeled

1 pt. red grape tomatoes, divided (about 20)

Round toothpicks, broken in half

1 medium cucumber

Melon baller

2 dressings or dips of choice (such as ranch or honey mustard)

Narrow platter (Sample uses a ceramic platter, 14″ long and 6½″ wide.)

Green kale, optional

To Begin...

1) Cut and chill radish tulips following the directions on page 39 or radish wheels following directions on page 52. If desired, make and chill celery curls from 2 stalks of celery according to directions on page 51.

2) Prepare green onion frills following the directions on page 40.

3) Parcook and chill asparagus spears according to directions on page 40.

4) Cut off each floret from the broccoli stalk; cover with damp paper towels and refrigerate.

5) To prepare bell pepper "pots," use a sharp knife to cut out the stem and core of each pepper; discard. Carve around top edge of peppers, following ridges to create a scalloped or zigzag edge. Carefully remove seeds and white membranes inside; rinse out hollow shells and drain on paper towels.

6) Cut remaining celery into 4″ to 4½″ lengths. Split the wide pieces into narrower sticks. Cut carrots to the same length, using the thickest end of each one. Split carrots in half lengthwise.

7) Insert a toothpick half into one end of 10 wide and 12 narrow celery sticks. Insert a toothpick half into the wide end of each carrot stick. Attach a radish tulip or wheel to the toothpick on the wide celery sticks and a grape tomato on the narrow celery sticks. Attach a broccoli floret to the toothpick on each carrot stick.

8) Cut 2 (2″) lengths from the center of the cucumber. With a melon baller, hollow out both pieces, leaving 1″ of flesh intact to form the bottom of each pot. Drain or pat dry with paper towels. Fill pots with dressing or dip.

9) Set peppers on the platter, trimming away bumps on the bottom as needed so pots will stand up. Fill yellow pepper with radish-celery tulips; fill green pepper with broccoli-carrot sticks and prepared onion frills. Fill red pepper with tomato-celery sticks and chilled asparagus spears. Set cucumber pots on platter and garnish with kale, celery frills and remaining tomatoes as desired.

No-Knead Bread Dough

(Yield: 2 pounds dough)

Use this recipe to make breadsticks, mini cinnamon rolls and round or standard loaves of bread. Prepare the basic dough below and then follow specific directions on bouquet pages to shape and bake as desired. Dough may be refrigerated for up to 5 days before shaping and baking.

1 (¼ oz.) pkg.
  granulated yeast

1½ tsp. salt

1 egg

¼ C. honey

2½ T. olive oil *or*
  vegetable oil

3 C. flour

½ C. whole wheat flour

1) In a large bowl, stir together 1 cup lukewarm water, yeast, salt, egg, honey and oil until blended. Mix in both flours until incorporated. Cover loosely and let rise at room temperature for about 2 hours.

2) Shape the dough immediately as desired and bake as directed, or cover and refrigerate for up to 5 days. To remove the quantity of dough needed for a recipe, simply dust with flour and cut off amount needed with kitchen shears or knife. Then refer to the following bouquet pages for shaping and baking. Refrigerate remaining dough and use it within 5 days.

Use this dough to:

- Shape and bake a round artisan loaf for **BLT Bouquet** on page 34.

- Shape and bake herbed breadsticks for **Escape to Capri** on page 16 or to garnish **Deli Delight** on page 50 or **Party Cheeseball** on page 60.

- Shape and bake mini cinnamon rolls for **On a Roll** bouquet on page 46.

Buttercream Frosting

(To frost cinnamon rolls on page 46.)

3 T. butter, softened

Dash of salt

½ tsp. vanilla extract

1 T. half & half

1¼ C. sifted powdered sugar

In a small bowl, beat together butter, salt, vanilla, half & half and powdered sugar until smooth and creamy. Spread frosting on cinnamon rolls with a knife or place frosting in a pastry bag fitted with a round tip and pipe frosting on rolls as desired. (Frosts 12 to 18 rolls)

Shrimp Filling

(Try this alternate filling for
Pinwheel Palooza on page 42.)

1 ripe avocado

4 oz. cream cheese, softened

¼ C. ketchup

1 T. prepared horseradish

1 tsp. finely grated lemon zest

2 T. lemon juice

½ tsp. chili powder

5 (10″) whole wheat or flour tortillas

3 C. shredded spinach leaves

⅔ C. smoked almonds, chopped

1 (4 oz.) can tiny shrimp, drained

Pit and dice avocado as directed on page 15. In a medium bowl, mash avocado flesh. Mix in cream cheese, ketchup, horseradish, lemon zest, lemon juice and chili powder until smooth and well-blended. Spread mixture over one side of tortillas. Top with a layer of spinach. Sprinkle evenly with almonds and shrimp. Roll up tortillas tightly and refrigerate for 30 minutes before slicing into pinwheels. (Fills 5 tortilla rolls)

Party Cheeseball

2 (8 oz.) pkgs. cream cheese, softened
¼ C. crushed pineapple, drained
2 T. finely chopped green bell pepper
2 T. finely chopped onion
2 tsp. seasoned salt
1 C. chopped pecans

Pretzel sticks, cracker sticks and/or breadsticks (purchased or homemade using recipe on page 58)
Crackers (such as Sociables)

1 In a medium bowl, mix cream cheese, pineapple, bell pepper, onion and seasoned salt until well blended. Shape mixture into a ball and roll in pecans. Chill for at least 1 hour.

2 Before serving, place cheeseball on a platter. Insert pretzels, cracker sticks and breadsticks as desired into crown of cheeseball. Insert crackers on edge around base of cheeseball. Serve promptly.

Variation:

After mixing cheeseball ingredients, form mixture into 1˝ balls. Roll balls in chopped pecans, crushed dried parsley or a mixture of pecans and parsley. Poke a pretzel stick into the top of each mini cheeseball and chill for 1 hour. Arrange cheeseballs on a serving platter surrounded by crackers.